Making
the Customer Experience
Magical
NOW!

How to Succeed In Business and Beat Out Your Competition Today!

Learn 9 Success Secrets:
Gain Employee Commitment
Attract More Customers
Create Customer Loyalty
Find and Hire Great People
Make the Workplace Fun
  And more...

JOHN FORMICA

America's Best Customer Experience Coach

www.johnformica.com

Advertising is how you buy customers.
Giving them an experience they will remember is how
you succeed in business today.

John Formica
(an "Ex-Disney Guy")
America's Best Customer Experience Coach

www.johnformica.com

November 2010

ISBN 978-0-9826526-6-4

Published by:
Desktop Wings Inc.
700 East Walnut Street
Perkasie, PA 18944
215-453-9312

 **Dedication**

This book is dedicated to my mom, Gabriella and my late dad, Thomas Formica, for instilling a lifetime core value of caring for and being kind to others. This core value was the foundation and influence for our family growing up and is still a value that my two loving sisters, Chris and Grace and I all live by today. I have no doubt that my parents' lifetime of caring actions and sincere kind spirit have affected and impacted the lives of many people in this world as well. Simply caring for others in a kind and helpful way, is an incredible and powerful message that any family, community, organization or business can all benefit from.

I would also like to give a heartfelt thank you to my loving and supporting wife Debbie along with my two sons, Adam and Eric. They have all made numerous and difficult sacrifices throughout my professional career. I will always be forever grateful for their encouragement, love, support and inspiration for writing and completing this book. I could not have done it without them. I also hope my boys see what is possible if you put your mind and effort into something, and use this book as a resource to guide them in their own professional careers.

Acknowledgments

An acknowledgment must go out to all of the millions and millions of small businesses in America and throughout the world. Their hard work and entrepreneurial spirit has always been my inspiration in becoming a small business owner and writing this book. From the person who was daring enough to sell everything they owned to start a business, to those who have a great new idea or service to provide a neighborhood community in need, I salute you.

I have to also acknowledge the many incredible small business owners that have helped and influenced me over the years. Special people like Ed Tubel, Owner of Sonny's BBQ Restaurants, who is a great mentor and friend with a wonderful and sincere passion to serve others; Lisa and Elston Howell, 4-Spoken Communication, who are fulfilling a dream of helping every unfortunate child to speak; Amy and Daniel Purifoy, DNA Conceptions, a marketing video and audio production company, whose mission to serve others goes well beyond their own business.

Kudos to the many Community College Small Business Center Directors in North Carolina who continue to share their wisdom, experience, and good counsel in helping entrepreneurs start and grow their own small businesses. Over the years, I have come to develop wonderful relationships and friendships with these particular directors: Ginger O'Neal, Bob Moore, Diane Finch, Lynn Davis, Fred Brooks, Cliff Ireland, Greg Hannibal, Tom Hemphill, John Smith, Doug Tarble, Georgette Chilton, Brenda Orders, Trudy Lynn, Deborah Hardison, Patricia Killette, Tamara Bryant, Lentz Stowe, Lynn Welborn, and a host of others. These Small Business Center Directors are all valuable assets and continue to make a difference in their county communities. Thank you all for giving me the opportunity to partner with you and present hundreds of seminars over the years, assisting thousands of small businesses and their employees with their training needs.

A special acknowledgment and heartfelt thank you goes out to Omega Sports in North Carolina. Their unique chain of sixteen small, customer-friendly running shoe sporting goods stores has been serving their communities since 1978. They are the best example of what a wonderful customer experience should be. I am sincerely grateful to have the opportunity to work with the leadership team of Regional Manager, Dan Keller and store managers Kurt Ringeling, Dave Wilson, and Irene Zimmerman. Their dedication to service and continued support for allowing me the opportunity to play a role at Omega Sports has truly been a rewarding and enjoyable experience.

To all small businesses that continue to be the foundation of building a wonderful America, I truly hope this book helps you make magic!

John Formica

www.johnformica.com

Table of Contents

Introduction

My goal in writing this book was to provide any small business with a simple handbook on how to make its customer experience and business culture magical. There have been other successful books written about Disney's success principles and how the company has become one of the most recognized experts on customer service. We all know that.

Share the Magic

What I wanted to do was share my personal 25-plus years of experience as a leader with the Walt Disney World Resort and other top service industry companies to help small businesses with their quest for creating a great — or what I call a "magical" — customer experience.

In the past seven years, I have delivered over 1,450 presentations to small businesses and professionals throughout the U.S. Many asked me about Disney's secrets of how they provide an incredible customer experience, "wow" their customers, and create a fun and positive work environment. "How does Disney do it?" Do you want to know the secret to Disney's success? I'll just give you the quick secret and you

don't have to bother reading the rest of this book.
Are you ready? Pixie dust! It's magical! They just
sprinkle pixie dust and everybody is happy. Really?

One person at one of my seminars said, "I know
what it is!" I asked, "You do?" "Yes, they must spike
the water in Orlando, Florida. That's why they built
all the theme parks there and everybody's happy!"

More than Pixie Dust

That is not it! Every business owner wishes it was
that simple. Disney has an incredible success model
that has worked for years. It continues to work and
it continues to be fine-tuned but it's not a secret! It's
not like the Kentucky Fried Chicken or Famous
Amos secret recipe that they try to hide and lock in a
vault!

There is no secret; it has much to do with Walt
Disney's original values, vision, and sure-sighted
management principles that create the magic. I
spent ten years with the Walt Disney World
company as a leader in the Resort Division, and
experienced firsthand the values and participated in
Disney's philosophy of "people management" to
achieve success.

While a manager at Disney's Yacht and Beach
Resort Hotel, my department had the highest guest
satisfaction ratings of all Disney operated hotels on
property. This prompted the Disney Institute,
Disney's Professional Development Seminars
Division, to contact me to find out how we did it. The

Institute was developing a new seminar on
"Customer Loyalty" and was looking for real
examples on how customer loyalty is created. My
department became one of their models for their new
seminar. I also had the opportunity to present a
small portion of the Disney Institute Seminar and
share my expertise to businesses and professionals
around the world.

One Simple Question

Today, through my keynote addresses, seminars,
team coaching, and speaking presentations, I share
those same success principles to help other
organization create magic. I challenge my audiences
with this single question; "If Disney can do it, why
can't you?" Understanding the true purpose of
engaging your employees' hearts, hiring the right
people, having a commitment to the details, and
creating a fun environment where your employees
have an opportunity to be successful, will all help
create a magical experience for your customers.

When I share how Disney does it, I often get a
response and reaction "Oh, I wish my company
would do that.", "Wow, can you share that with my
boss.", or "I only run a small business and I wish I
had the resources that Disney has." Or even better,
"That only applies to large companies." Yet when I
breakdown the Disney model to small business
owners, they realize that these success principles
can be applied to their own businesses as well.

Proof that the Model Works

How do I know Disney's model works? I have
personally applied the model to two organizations
that I worked for after I left Disney. The first
example is a hotel that I managed just after leaving
the Disney organization. This hotel was so poorly
operated, it was often called a "sock hotel". Do you
know what a "sock hotel" is? It is a hotel whose guest
rooms are so bad that the guests choose to leave
their socks on in the room. After two years, applying
the model, the hotel received the Pinnacle Award for
being one of the top convention hotels in the state of
North Carolina.

I then applied the model as an Executive Director of
an assisted living organization that was on
probation. It was about 45% occupied and given a
"D" score rating on its last resident feedback
questionnaire. After two years applying the model,
the facility received an "A" rating, occupancy
reached 90%, and it had a much better
recommendation rating from local doctors who
referred residents to the facility.

This model works particularly in small businesses,
where results can be noticed by customers and
employees in just one day. Imagine what your
business would look like if you applied the model
and saw immediate results of happier customers.
What would that do for your business?

The Heart and Soul of the Country

I truly believe that small business is the foundation and the heart and soul of this country. Dan Danner, president and CEO of the National Federation of Independent Business, agrees in his statement, "Small business owners start and build businesses, creating most of this country's new jobs along the way. What some people fail to realize is small businesses also contribute millions of dollars in money, in-kind contributions and time to local charities, service clubs, youth groups and more." Entrepreneurship in these businesses has always been the strongest engine of our economy.

Today, studies show that small businesses of fewer than 500 employees represent just over 99% of the almost 30 million businesses in America. They employ over half of the U.S. jobs, employing 60 million people, and have generated 64% of new jobs over the past 15 years. The success of small business in America will be the key turning point for our economy here in the US and throughout the world. That is why I have such a strong passion to help the small business owner.

Need to Be Nimble

Every day, we see that large companies are struggling and are having a difficult time competing in this changing economy. Some are too big to make quick changes that are necessary today. It is like a big cruise ship trying to turn around in the ocean. The turn is slow and gradual. How much time does

it take for the ship to make the adjustment?
Remember the Titanic? Small ships and speed boats
on the other hand are able to make quick maneuvers
and adjust to change direction in less time.

The same goes for what I call creating a magical
customer experience. Many large companies have
taken the customer experience for granted and are
taking too long to make the necessary changes to
compete in this challenging economy.

I was once sharing what I do with a high level leader
of a large company and how I might be able to help
his organization create a better customer experience.
He of course loved the Disney model and agreed that
I could help but his response was that they had
already started a new corporate customer service
directive in the last three years. They had invested a
lot of time and labor; it would be too costly to start a
new initiative. Can you imagine a customer service
program taking three or more years to be
implemented? What about a typical small business?
Do you think a small business owner could survive if
it took three years to implement the necessary
changes in order to give their customers what they
want, change a menu in a restaurant, come up with
new ways to be more competitive in the market, or
give better service? We all know what a disaster that
circumstance would lead to.

Simple Success Principles

I suggest you use this book as an action guide to help
you, your staff, and your business be more like

Disney in its quest to provide a magical customer experience. It is not rocket science or some new and expensive corporate change agent or initiative. These are just simple success principles that I learned while being a hotel manager with the Walt Disney World Resort.

I have personally used these principles and have been successful in helping others do the same. Today, through my team coaching and seminars many small businesses have utilized these success principles in their own business and have seen some great magical results. I believe you can, too.

John teaches several seminars to very large audiences at the college. He is very dynamic and a knowledgeable presenter. Small businesses and students often call to ask when John is coming back! Patricia Killette, Director, Small Business Center, Wilson Community College, NC

Chapter 1:
Create the Dream

I spent more than 25 years managing and
supervising people in the hotel and service industry.
I was very fortunate to work for some pretty
successful companies like Hyatt Hotels, Hilton, and
especially the Walt Disney World Resort Company.
As I travel around the U.S. many people say to me,
"Wow! Working for Disney must have been a really
neat job! I've always dreamed of working for
Disney!"

Mickey Mouse is not just that cuddly little cute
character that you're familiar with. The Mickey
Organization—or as we used to call it, the Mouse
House—was probably the most challenging job I ever
had. If you have ever been to Disney World, you
know that the expectations are extremely high and
you probably wondered "how do they do it day in and
day out?"

You might not know this, but today there are almost
50,000 employees that work for the Disney World
Resort in Orlando Florida. It's one of the largest
single -location employers in the U.S. When we visit
Disney, their employees or as Disney calls them, cast
members, all seem to come to work smiling, happy
and excited to be there. If they see a paper on the

floor or something out of place, they immediately run to pick the paper up or quickly correct the situation.

In your organization or business, why can't you get people to show up to work on time, answer the phones, or be productive? How does Disney do it? Let's begin with what I think is one of their core success principles.

Mission Statements Alone Don't Work

How many of you have mission statements? Yes, I know, most companies have eloquent mission statements. Can you recite yours? Probably not and I guess your employees couldn't recite it either. I must tell you. I am not a big fan of mission statements. I am not telling you to throw yours away or that they are a waste of time. Mission statements do serve a purpose but not what most companies think.

When I work with companies or do team coaching, one of the first things I like to do is to go walking around the organization, talking to employees. I always ask them, "Can you recite your mission statement?" They usually say, "Huh?" Most can't tell me or try and put some words together that sound like one. Employees often tell me that they don't remember them because they are either too long or the mission statement often changes. One employee once told me, "I don't know, we had this big rally six months ago, we got these big balloons and coffee mugs, but my coffee mug broke and I don't know what my mission statement is any more." Many are forced by their managers to memorize them. Any of these sound familiar? Just ask your own employees and see what they say about your mission statement.

Mission statements are usually big vision plans that tell me how, when or what the organization would like to achieve. I think those are all import goals and objectives for any company.

Every business needs to have a vision and goals, but to the hourly employee, they could care less about the what, how or when. For example, as a business, you might have a goal to be the number one business in the southeastern United States! That's nice but who really cares besides you? I certainly don't care if I work there! Why? As an employee, do I get anything if we are number one? I might get to raise the banner and say "WE ARE NUMBER ONE!" High five! Then I go back to work only to be told by my manager that I am expected to work even harder to stay number one.

We all know what the consequences are if you don't remain number one. Do lots of finger pointing, blaming, new policies, rule changes, threats, punishments, getting yelled at by managers... sound familiar? All because of some leader at the top of the food chain's ego is being disappointed. I am sure many of you have experienced this before. That's why I believe most mission statements alone don't work.

What is Your Purpose?

Let me share one of Disney's most important success principles that will help make magic in your business.

First you must define your purpose. This is more than just quoting your mission statement.

Defining the purpose is why I think Disney is so successful. Can you tell me Disney's purpose? Most people when asked the question during my presentations can usually tell me in a matter of seconds. "Make people happy!" they shout out. How come the participants in the seminar can tell me what Disney's employee's purpose is but many do not even know the purpose of the business for which they spend 40 hours a week working? It is simple. The Disney organization has never taken their "purpose" lightly, particularly in sharing Walt's vision.

I have a challenge for you the next time you go to Disney World. Whether you are staying in a Disney hotel, or you are in one of the theme parks, please go and ask any of the 50,000 cast members that work there, "What is your purpose?" They will quickly tell you, "To make people happy!" They know exactly what it is. Try it!

How do they do it? It is simple. Every new hire, whether they are an hourly employee such as a housekeeper or a top executive must spend two days in "Traditions" training before they are permitted to begin the assigned role for which they were hired.

This orientation program introduces the values and true purpose of every Disney worker. It's not an orientation where you learn about your benefits or what the policy is for calling in sick or where to park your car. It's nothing like that. It's all about understanding the values of Walt Disney himself and the sole purpose of your role to make people happy. In other words, no matter what the job role is, the purpose always remains the same: "To make people happy!" After returning from their "Traditions" training, employees are often looked at to be "Disney-ized" into understanding the purpose.

Shortly after joining the Disney organization, I was a manager at Disney's Contemporary Resort and needed a new hire to start right away. We had a large convention group arriving in a few weeks and I needed my new staff to be trained and ready for their arrival. I suggested that the new hire begin his training now and go to Traditions training next month when it was offered again. I was strongly told "no". All cast members must first go through "traditions" training, before they are allowed to start their job. I said to myself, "Why is this company so darned structured?" I would come to realize it shortly after the new hire returned from his two days of "Traditions" training. He was full of energy, excitement and of course driven by his purpose. The new hire would never lose sight of that sole purpose—to make people happy—while he worked at my hotel.

Okay, so the question I will ask you is this: "What does your orientation program look like?" Do you show a short, outdated non-purpose driven video that you rush people through as fast as possible just get that warm body started?" Okay, I realize it would cost a small business a fortune to put every single new hire through an extra 16 hours of training. It doesn't have to be 16 hours. The amount of time is not important. It is the quality that you place at the beginning of the hiring process, defining the true purpose as to why your business exists is most important. That is how you begin to create the dream.

Magical Action Plan: Look at Your Employee Orientation Program

1. What is your current employee orientation?

_____

_____

_____

_____

2. How does it train your employees to understand your company's **purpose**, or does it just focus on policies and procedures?

_____

_____

_____

_____

Chapter 2:
Purpose Is
More Important
Than the Job

Have you ever seen a Disney employee stop what they are doing and take a picture of an entire family in front of the Magic Kingdom castle? Why do they do that? To make people happy! Let me explain further.

Let's say I am a cast member at Disney with a dustpan and broom and I am assigned an area of the Magic Kingdom. I receive a job description with instructions and training. What is my job? To pick up trash and keep my assigned area of the Magic Kingdom clean. Right! Now what is my purpose? To make people happy! Right again! While I am doing my job, I always have my radar up looking for ways to make people happy. One way is to offer to take a picture of a family in front of the castle. Would that make you happy? Of course! There is no policy, job description, or boss that says I am supposed to take 50 pictures a day. I do it because I want to. I never lose sight of the purpose.

Let me put this in a real life and true Disney perspective. Think about how your business or organization might react and handle this scenario. Again, let say I am walking around with my dustpan and broom and an elderly couple comes up to me and asks. "Excuse me, we know that you work here but can you show us how to get to the Fantasyland?" I say, "Sure, you just take the walkway, it's in one big circle and you will eventually get to Fantasyland." The elderly couple appears to be confused and nervous and states, "Um, we don't know. We tried to go that way but there were a lot of people and we're not really sure how far to go." As a Disney cast member, what am I thinking? I should take them there, right! Absolutely!

If I escort them to Fantasyland it would make them happy. So I put down my dustpan and broom and escort them to Fantasyland. Now, while I am doing that I am always looking for other ways to make them happy. I ask, "Are you going to go to the parade today?" The couple says, "Yes." I say, "Remember, it starts at 3 o'clock. You see that spot over there, in that corner? Get there about 2:30pm; it's one of the best spots in the whole park to see the parade." I begin to learn about their grandchildren and they are learning about my wife and my kids.

When I finally get them to Fantasyland, they are all excited and happy. They are no longer fearful, and what else happened? The couple has just made a new friend. When they return to their home town, who are they going to talk about? Me! I am their newfound Disney friend who made them happy. I created a friendship and a relationship because I never lost sight of the purpose.

But I also remember I still have a J-O-B and I have to get back to my original work location. So I go hustling all the way back to my workstation area and I can't find my dustpan and broom. Where is it? I look over, and my boss has the dustpan and broom and he is sweeping away. What does my boss at Disney World say to me? "Great job! You were doing what, John? You helped that elderly couple and escorted them all the way, and were they happy?" I say, "Absolutely! They really appreciated it."

My boss then tells me that he is going to put my name in the next newsletter. He might give me a little card to turn into the gift shop for a prize. He also tells me that his going to announce my name and share my experience at the next staff meeting. Wow! Am I excited! Why is my boss making a big deal out of it? At Disney the purpose always comes before the job. Always! Unless it's a safety or a security issue, then those obviously take preference.

What would most bosses do and say in that situation? How would you handle it? What would you have said to me, your employee, when I returned to my work location? Would this sound familiar? "Where have you been? What are you doing John? There must be a million people in the park today; are you are going to escort everyone who needs directions? We have to keep this place clean and I am busy doing your job! Maybe we don't really need you!"

If you react that way, what do you think happens next? How do you think your employee feels after hearing your critical feedback? What apparently becomes more important to the employee? The J-O-

B. Why should I or other employees want to make people happy when we know that we are going to get chewed out? See the disconnection? The purpose has to be reinforced and positively supported from all levels of your organization.

There are policies and job descriptions that tell Disney employees what to do. However, employees are not being babysat or controlled by a boss. Not at all. They do it because they want to do it and because they never lose sight of their purpose. So they take pictures, leave designated work areas if appropriate to escort guests and do other wonderful things to make people happy each and every day.

We all know that Disney employees are recognized and appreciated for examples of creating magic while at work. It is more than just a phrase; it is an uncompromising value that makes a Disney employee special. They are truly passionate about their purpose. If your employees truly understand their purpose, you will find more commitment and passion on their part to "want" to do a great job rather than feel that they "have" to do it. The key is to create an emotional attachment and engage the hearts of your employees, and tie it to the purpose.

Can Purpose Work with Any Organization?

I believe purposeful work exists in any organization or business. In fact, once you begin engaging the hearts of your employees in any organization you then can begin to make magic. For example, during one of my presentations, a participant stated that this purpose philosophy might work at a theme park or resort but not in a small manufacturing company which produced bolts. Obviously, not as exciting as Disney, but to make my point, I ask him what was the purpose of making the bolts and where did the bolts go after being produced. In other words, what was the purpose?

He shared with me that the purpose was to make good quality bolts to be used in the landing gear of airplanes. I then asked him what would happen if the bolts were not made properly or of poor quality? He said that the landing gear would not function properly. I asked again, what happens if the landing gear does not function properly? He stated that it might cause a crash landing. Then what might happen if the plane crashes? People might get hurt. After further discussion, I asked, so what is the true purpose of your bolt-making company? Take that message to your entire staff and ask them what their purpose is at the plant. He got back to me a week later and was excited to tell me their new purpose: "To protect and save lives during landing."

What a perfect purpose! Rather than to just create quality bolts and increase shareholder value, typically found in "Mission Statements", the employees now have a true purpose to get passionate and excited about. Who wouldn't want to make great quality bolts at work to protect and save lives? Actually the plant's productivity and efficiency increased after just implementing and creating a meaningful purpose. Now that is a "magical" result.

Purposeful work can be found in any organization, business, school, health care or team.

I was a keynote speaker at a conference for professional educators with 300 teachers in the audience. During my presentation, I asked the teachers, "What is your purpose?" What do you think they told me? To teach and educate students! Participants in the audience shouted out additional examples such as, "to prepare students for college, help them graduate and even give them lifelong skills." I responded by asking the audience, "Is that really your purpose or is it your job? Do my two sons actually need teachers to help them graduate, get them into college, or to give them lifelong skills?" We all of course know how important teachers are and instrumental in their facilitating role by teaching the information necessary to pass and get ahead. But do I need a teacher to do it?

Of course, I had to prepare myself because I was about to get thrown off the stage by many of them. Then I asked the most important question. "Why did you get into teaching in the first place?" What did they tell me? "Summers off!" one teacher shouted out. We all got a good laugh.

Seriously, why do people get into teaching? Some of the answers were along these lines: to inspire, to make a difference! And make a difference to whom? Kids! They love children and they want to make a difference in their lives. What a meaningful purpose! I then shared, "If you truly believed in that purpose every single day, what will your lesson plans or

classroom environment look like? Would you go to
work on Mondays saying, "I can't wait till Friday.",
or "How long before the summer?"

When you keep your mind and actions on the
purpose, everything else will fall into place. People
are more inspired by the why, the reason for doing
it, and making a difference in a life of a child is
certainly a worthy purpose.

When I ask audiences, "What is the purpose of the
employees at Disney?" Most say, "To make a profit."
That is not the purpose. That is the successful
outcome from making people happy. Just as
increased productivity and efficiency is the outcome
from protecting and saving lives at landing, and
graduating, preparing, teaching, and educating our
children is the outcome of the purposeful work as a
teacher. Whether you are a business owner,
manager or supervisor, isn't it much easier to lead
and manage people who want to be there rather
than those who don't?

"Purposeful work means you are passionate about
what you do, because you want to, not because you
have to."

Develop a Magical Purpose.

Your goal as a leader, coach or organization is to
help your employees create and define the purpose of
what is truly emotional and meaningful in their
daily jobs. This cannot be shared in an informal,
quick, get-it-over-with orientation program that

many companies force upon their new hires.
Companies that are successful have meaningful,
organized, committed, and purposeful orientation
programs that share the true and uncompromising
values of their company.

Take a tip from Walt Disney; once your purpose is
defined, recognized, rewarded, and emotionally
purposeful, your employees will be more committed
and excited to do a job that they want to do and not
feel as though they have to. Walt Disney said it best,
"When you believe in a thing, believe in it all the
way, implicitly and unquestionably." In business, if
you make your purpose believable and
unquestionable to your employees, you too can
create magic. Here are some tips in creating a
meaningful purpose in your small business.

Purposeful Facts: (The "why")

To be effective, your company's purpose:

- Must be important and inspiring to capture
  the soul of your business or organization.
- Should not require external motivation or
  justification.
- Gets at a deeper reason for your company's
  existence.
- Should not be confused with specific goals or
  business strategies.
- Should be long lasting and resilient to
  change.

Here are a few business examples:

Mary Kay: "To give unlimited opportunity to women."

Wal-Mart: "To save money and live better."

Regina Medical Birthing Center: "Our family caring for yours."

County Housing Authority: "To provide hope and opportunity to all in need."

Assisted Living and Skilled Nursing: "To provide trust, compassionate care

Sonny's Barbeque: "Passion to Serve"

The next step is to create your own magical purpose for your company.

Magical Action Plan: Create Your Own Magical Purpose

You can't just pull your magical purpose out of a hat. Here are some tips to help you create a process that will lead to a purpose that will help your company.

- Get as many people involved in developing the statement, such as business owners, managers, supervisors, clerical staff and front line staff.
- Don't be afraid to get feedback from your loyal customers or clients.
- Ask each other "Why is that important?" at least five times before settling on a purpose.
- Make it clear, short and easy to understand.
- Make it emotional.
- Make it visible and memorable.
- Reward and recognize people when it is carried out.
- Post accomplishments everywhere and discuss at meetings.
- Celebrate successes and have fun!

Chapter 3:
People Make the
Magic

Would you agree that in any business, people are our greatest asset? It is not what we do; it is what our employees do that make managers successful and businesses magical. The success of any company is only as good as the people who perform the jobs. Our people control a lot of other things as well.

Have you ever known a small business or manager whose career crashed or business sunk because they hired the wrong people? Businesses and career failures often can be traced back to the inability to recruit, interview, and select employees. The truth is that our people influence our career and business growth. They influence our performance evaluations, bonuses, pay raises and even the amount of money that we make in our lifetime. How's that for influence? Should we look at that greatest asset a little more closely? You bet!

Small businesses spend thousands of dollars on advertising, branding, beautiful store fronts, attractive web-site, and all kinds of marketing materials. But all of that means nothing if they don't have great people working there.

If that greatest asset is so important to our success, why do we take the hiring process for granted? Jim Collins, in his book *Good to Great* describes how "getting the right people on the bus, the wrong people off the bus, and placing the right people on the bus in the right seats," will leap companies to greatness. Ask yourself how closely do you and your business follow Jim Collins' simple but incredible advice.

Find People to Fill Roles Not Just Positions

Do you have the right people in your business, organization or team to make magic? If you have the wrong people working for you, then no seminar, book, training or implementing all the purposes in the world will make magic. If you don't have the right people to do it, it just won't work.

How many times have you been out as a customer and you said to yourself, "That person is just right for that job or position"? The Disney organization is a perfect example where its employees play a specific role in the show. That is no coincidence. Disney hires people to fill roles, not positions! They always seem to have the right people working there. Yet, how many businesses have you been to where people—or should I call them "warm bodies"—are working in positions that don't match personalities, skills, attitudes, or energy. Was that hiring process taken for granted? Did the warm body mentality kick in?

What alternative do we have? We need people to perform tasks effectively, complete paperwork accurately, and serve our customers. If not, our bosses and customers will certainly complain. But they complain anyway due to poor service and a lack of a caring attitude. Guess who pays for those complaints? Your business!

Many small businesses seem to place a warm body in a position because they need to fill that position. This is done without regard as to how that person may affect the customer experience, answer the phone, greet customers, or create customer loyalty. I have even seen companies promote people into management positions because they think it might work out. We all know what can happen if we put people in the wrong role. Very little magic occurs. You might get away with it in the short term, but it just doesn't work and probably not worth the risk.

Finding the Right Person is Like Casting the Right Actor

Let me give you a perfect example. My wife and kids are big fans of the sitcom *Seinfeld*. My favorite character in *Seinfeld* is George Costanza. His real name is Jason Alexander and he played various parts before *Seinfeld*, but the show certainly helped his reputation.

Jason Alexander is an incredible actor. Did you know that he sang and danced on Broadway and won a Tony award? He also was nominated for an Emmy seven times for his role on *Seinfeld*. There aren't too many actors or actresses who have been nominated for both of these awards. When you need an actor, why aren't you automatically going to choose Jason Alexander? Just look at his resume! Don't we look at resumes when we try to hire people? Don't we look at applications? They're so impressive!

However, if you want to hire someone to play the part of James Bond, are you going to hire Jason Alexander? Why not? Most women would agree that they would have little desire to see Jason Alexander coming out of the ocean in a swimsuit. However the new Bond is a different story. Okay! The point is, Jason Alexander is a very good actor, but he is not ideal for every role.

One summer, my calendar and schedule were fairly light. My two boys were going away to summer camp for most of the summer, so I thought I would look for a part time summer job to stay busy. My goal was to find a customer service position in a business that I liked. Being an avid runner, a former soccer player at a Division 1 college, and a sports enthusiast, I decided to apply at my favorite running/sporting goods store, Omega Sports. Omega Sports is a family run small business with 16 locations throughout North Carolina. Their stores are relatively small but are very customer focused because of their size and loyal following.

I had come to know the store manager, Kurt. I was the friendly, outgoing, and loyal customer who was very knowledgeable about running. From our many conversations, Kurt also knew that I coached and presented customer service seminars and workshops. When I first asked Kurt if he was hiring he replied "When can you start?" He knew that I would be in a perfect role and that was exactly what he was looking for in a potential employee. He just about hired me on the spot.

To me, working there is not a job. Why? I love sports, and as an avid runner, I want to help people find the right running shoes to avoid possible injuries. I also enjoy helping parents and children pick out the best soccer cleats that fit and are at the right price. Especially if they are playing soccer for the first time? Wow! That's exciting! I often get on my knees and have fun conversations with their children, while fitting them in the right soccer cleats.

I ask them to remember John who sold you the "magic" shoes that scores goals! "Really?" They say. "Oh yes!" I tell them to come back and tell me when they score a goal. I have kids later returning to the store saying, "Mr. John, Mr. John, I scored a goal!" I give them high fives and say, "Way to go!" I sometimes even give them little stickers with smiley faces. I truly have fun doing it.

Kurt, the manager, and other staff members often ask me if I am always this cheery and where I get all the energy. There are no secrets. I am just in the right role, with a great organization, that allows me the opportunity to be myself, have fun and do whatever is necessary to make the customer happy.

I usually don't see the big box stores giving personal attention and service that a small business like

Omega Sports provides. The goal is not to just hire people who need a job, but to hire people who believe in what you believe.

If you have a quiet, introverted person, and you put them in the wrong role by working in your reception area or front desk, answering phones or greeting your customers with a methodical monotone voice, what type of experience will your customers receive? That is simply not going to work. Yet how many times have you visited a store, restaurant or business and you are greeted by something close to a dead fish?! No eye contact, staring down at a computer with no sense of urgency in welcoming you.

Or better yet, I ask them "How are you today?" and I get a lethargic and disappointing response back such as "Fine. It's almost Friday." Or "I'm really tired. I was out late last night and thank goodness I only have a few hours left." Or "It is going to be a long day because we are short staffed today." What does that tell me about their employees or business? Your success in business rests on the shoulders of these reluctant employees. Not much magic going on there.

The person that you hire or bring on board might be a good person, but are they in the wrong role? Are they best suited for their role in your business? That's why you have to be very selective. To be selective means you have to make sure you get the right people on the bus.

Many business owners, particularly in a small business, don't take the hiring and selection process seriously. A family member or relative who needs a job is often hired in a small business with disregard to whether they are the right fit for their role. Again, the goal is not to just hire people who need a job. It is to hire people who believe what you believe. It can make all the difference.

The fact is that most business owners are never taught how to hire the right people, or ever get to learn and practice interviewing skills. Many companies and managers foolishly conclude that "you can't find good people anymore." The truth is that they are out there. You just have to learn to be creative in finding and selecting them. When your business success and career depends on it, hiring is not something you can leave to the HR department or the sales people at Monster.com. You must become better and involved. Schedule a workshop or attend one in your area or pickup a book at the library or local bookstore. When you become skilled, knowledgeable and involved in the recruitment processes, your business will surely benefit.

Here are some simple tips on finding and selecting the right people.

1. Always be on the lookout for magical customer-service friendly or ideal people

Customers will always remember people over product or service.

We are all customers. How many times have you
visited a restaurant and seen someone who is really
friendly, bubbly and outgoing? Don't we say to
ourselves, "Boy, we really could use someone like
that in our organization!" What is stopping you from
asking? Just go and talk to the person. First,
acknowledge them and tell them they are doing a
great job. Point out that you've noticed it and then
say, "In our company, we're always looking for good
people like you, do you know anybody? Do you have
any brothers and sisters that are just like you?" And
guess what they might say?

They might say no, they might suggest a few people
they know, or you might plant a seed that someday
they might say "Yes, what about me?"

One of the best hires I've ever had in my entire
career at Hyatt Hotels came from a Dunkin Donuts
coffee shop. Her name was Gloria and she was
unbelievable! She was one of the most friendly,
customer-service focused individuals I have ever
met. She created magic in that coffee shop and I
needed her to create magic at my front desk. So I
stole her right out of the coffee shop and gave her an
opportunity at my hotel's front desk. We could teach
her about the hotel but you can't teach someone how
to be customer friendly. We didn't have to because
she was a natural. In fact, she won the Employee of
the Year award by getting every single vote. Great
people are out there. You just have to find them

2. Don't wait until you have an opening.

Most businesses wait until they have an opening and then start the process. If you do, you will be in a reactive mode, and that never works. You need to have a whole pool of people that you can call, you've already witnessed in action, interviewed, screened, and referenced checked, and that you're already excited about. Just keep in touch with them. When you have an opening position available, you contact them and if they are still willing to join your business, they give their two weeks notice and you've got them: a great hire!

3. Get out of your office to interview.

I don't know why we interview people in our offices. Is that where they work? Do they work in your office? Of course not! Put them in the environment where they will actually be working in and observe how they perform. Especially in customer service!

Walk them around your business! See how they interact with fellow employees and customers. Do they have eye contact? Do they open up doors? Are they willing to stick their hand out and say, "Hi, my name is Suzie; I am applying for a job here." Do they pick up pieces of paper? Do they have energy and enthusiasm? Do they acknowledge people in the hallways? Can you picture them working for you and would they be a good fit in your business?

Magical Action Plan: Finding and Hiring Magical People

What role is the person playing in that particular position? What absolute qualities must the person have to fit in that role?

List those qualities and then go out and find and hire people with those particular qualities.

_____

_____

_____

_____

_____

_____

_____

_____

Chapter 4:
What Do Your
Customers
Really Want?

Do you know what your customers want? I mean really want? I hope so. The fact is that most businesses don't.

Businesses think they know. Many base their decisions on feedback from a few strong opinionated customers, neighbors, family members or staff. I am not saying that these people's viewpoint of your business is not important or valuable. But how do you really know?

The problem is that only 4% of customers will complain or give you feedback. Most businesses brush that feedback aside thinking the customer is just a complainer or wants something for free. If you want to know what your customers really want, you have to think like your customer. Put yourself in their shoes.

Understand the Mindset of Your Customers

People don't care how much you know until they know how much you care.
Theodore Roosevelt

When I first joined the Disney organization, they were operating only five hotels including the Fort Wilderness Campground. Disney was in the process of expanding their portfolio of Disney hotels and was building two new hotels: the Grand Floridian Beach Resort and the Caribbean Beach Resort. Prior to working at Disney, I was a manager with Hyatt Hotels in Washington DC and in Chicago. The hotels in those cities were in highly competitive markets, always fighting to gain their share of transient business professionals and conventions.

When I joined Disney, their five existing hotels experienced 95% occupancy or better with very little competition among the other hotels in the Orlando area. These occupancy numbers were unheard of in normal hotels throughout the country. I remember telling a long term hotel Disney manager how lucky Disney was that they had little or no competition.

This particular Disney manager asked me who I thought was Disney's competition. I shared other hotels such as Marriott, Hilton, Hyatt, and the Peabody Hotel in the area but knew they were no match to compete with Disney because all of those hotels were outside the Disney property. He replied, although those hotels I mentioned were competitive hotels, Disney's competition is much more than just hotels. Disney's competition could be anyone. In other words, any company that satisfies customers better than Disney now becomes Disney's competition.

It dawned on me that he was right. Customers not only judge and compare their overall experience with your business, they also compare how someone answers the phone, takes your order, greets you at the door, solves a problem, or goes out of their way to help you. Your competition is no longer just in your industry or similar business, your competition is literally anyone who your customers come in contact with.

Do you know who your competition is? If you are in the printing business your competition goes beyond other print shops. The same goes for landscaping businesses, restaurants, banks, dentist offices, craft shops, retail stores, etc. The fact is that everyone is your competition. Most people and customers make a mental picture in their minds of how a person should be treated and that becomes the standard by which their experience is judged.

What does that mean to the small business owner? If you have a person answering the phone, I am going to compare that person and my experience with anyone else who has ever answered a phone. My comparison may not even be a business similar to yours. I might compare it to a person who answered a phone incredibly well at a local school, church, or totally different business.

Here's an example. Melissa is an assistant at my Nationwide Insurance Agency office in Charlotte, NC. She has a wonderful, pleasant, and cheerful voice every time I call the office. I always judge other phone conversations based on my experience with

Melissa. She is consistent and always provides me with a positive experience. After calling any business I always ask myself, "How come they don't have people like Melissa answering the phone for their business? Why isn't the person cheery when they answer? Why do they sound like they are reading from a script? Why do they rush the call? How come I get the impression that they don't really seem to care?"

Melissa comes across as sincere with the right tone, and seems genuinely concerned about the person calling. Why? She knows that when most people call their insurance agency it is usually because of some sort of need or emergency. She anticipates the caller's anxiety immediately and is sincerely concerned about helping.

Why can't all businesses do that? You may not be in the insurance business but you are in the service business. The same comparison applies to your front doors, parking lots, restrooms, how calls get transferred, and so on. Your customers are comparing you with other business and organizations, whether they are in your industry or not.

If you ship parts across America and it takes more than two days for your customers to receive the part, your customers will compare you with FedEx. Why? FedEx will guarantee its delivery by 10:30 am the next day and you don't. In other words, FedEx cares and your company doesn't.

If my doctor's office calls me the next day and asks how I am feeling, I am going to compare them with other businesses where I spent thousands of dollars and who don't call, send a note, or thank me for such a large purchase. It is all about perception. What do you really want as a customer? Customers desire a personal connection and to feel that you care. It is plain and simple. Here is what customers really want.

What Customers Really Want!

- They desire a *personal* connection and attention.
- They want *reliability*, and to know that you will provide what you promised.
- They want you to be *responsive* to their needs and willing to help.
- They want *assurance* that they are getting what they paid for, and they made the right choice to do business with you.
- They want you to *empathize* with their feelings, frustrations, sorrows, anxiety, and excitement.
- They want certain *tangibles* and have expectations of cleanliness, appearance, atmosphere, operating equipment.
- They want to be *wowed* or surprised.

Most of all customers want an *experience* they feel they can share with friends, family, coworkers, neighbors, and people they meet on the street. In other words, your customers want to be able to brag about you and your business. They want to tell everyone they know how you gave them personal attention and responded to their needs without being asked. They appreciate the fact that your staff empathized with their challenges, frustrations, and feelings as if they were their own. They tell everyone how they specially were treated and how they can't wait to go back. This is very similar to the experience they receive when visiting Walt Disney World. People come back from their trip to Disney and can't wait to tell their friends about their wonderful and magical experiences.

Do your customers talk about you and your business that way? They should. Customers just don't crave service, they crave an experience they can talk about and rave as much as they do in telling you about a great movie, recipe, or young child's experience at school or ballgame.

It Is Not About the Coffee

I enjoy visiting my local Starbucks in the morning but it is not about the coffee. Oh, I look forward to ordering a tall simmering hot cup of coffee but that is not the only reason why I go there. I am certainly capable of making my own cup of Starbucks coffee at home.

So why do I go to Starbucks? For the experience. If I am at home and not traveling, I like to take my net-book into my neighborhood Starbucks, order a tall black coffee, sit down at a comfortable table or couch, and work. I guess you call it work. It certainly doesn't feel like work. Meeting people, listening to small talk conversations and networking with other professionals is not really work. However, it has become a staple in building my business.

Starbucks offers me a professional environment with other business professionals who have shared needs, challenges and successes, all of whom are potential new clients of mine. Some have helped me with advice on marketing, web site designs, and good books to read. It is not about the coffee. It is about the experience that I receive while I am there.

Today, McDonalds claims to have better coffee at a cheaper price. However, I have no interest in sitting in a McDonalds with my net-book, hanging around screaming kids and smelling like French fries when I leave. Don't get me wrong, I really like McDonalds too. I just choose to go there when I want a different experience. It all boils down to what I want—an experience—which becomes more important to me than my need for coffee.

Wants vs. Needs: Is There a Difference?

In any business, it is valuably important to understand the needs and wants of your customers. The question to ask is there a difference between needs and wants of your customers? Can it be different? The answer is yes. The needs and wants of your customers can be very different.

What do you think people need when they go to Disney World, besides lots of money, energy and a comfortable pair of shoes? Most people who visit Disney World need a vacation to relax, recharge their batteries, refrain from cooking, and enjoy amenities that they don't normally have at home. That very well might be what they need. But what do they want when they visit Walt Disney World? They want a great experience, different than what they can receive anywhere else. It is not about the rides or food or hotel beds. It is about the vacation experience that Disney provides them while they are there.

This was my challenge as a Disney Resort manager. It was a constant challenge to exceed the expectations of our guests each and every day, and to give them an experience that they wanted but not necessarily needed. Perhaps this is the very reason why some guests chose to stay at a Disney Resort Hotel rather than a surrounding hotel in the Orlando area. Isn't this the same challenge for any small business?

Magical Action Plan:
Your Customers'
Needs and Wants

Make a list of what you and your staff think that your customers *need* when they visit your business. For example, your list might include food or beverage, clothing, jewelry, materials and supplies, information, questions answered, etc. Then make a list of what you think they **really want** when they visit your business. What experience are they seeking? Put yourself in your customers' shoes. Do they need food to satisfy their hunger or do you want really appeasing, good tasting food that will melt in their mouth? Do they need new clothes or are they looking for an attractive outfit recommended by a helpful clerk that will flatter their appearance? Challenge each team member to come up with what they believe are unique wants from a customer's point of view and then find ways or strategies to fulfill them.

_____

_____

_____

_____

Chapter 5:
Listening to
Your Customers is
Magical

You don't build the product for yourself. You need to know what the people want and build it for them.
Walt Disney

I have partnered with numerous businesses—large and small—with my "Customer Experience Makeover Coaching Programs" that I developed. It is a very simple and effective service that I offer to help evaluate a business's existing customer experience. The entire customer experience is evaluated from phone calls, emails, walking in and snooping around in general, observing what goes on in the business. I spend time talking to employees, managers, customers, the competition, and even the people in the community.

My goal is not to just find all the issues that result in a less desirable experience, but to report what a customer's perception might be from their experience. I receive great feedback from staff and customers, as well as details about the company's reputation in the community. I like to call it the sights, sounds, and smells of the customer experience.

Most people think the term "sights" just covers evaluating the cleanliness of the business. However, "sights" can also evaluate workers text messaging or burying their heads in a computer rather than making themselves available to help or assist a customer. I might visually witness staff avoiding customers when they first enter the business without acknowledging or saying a simple hello. Worse yet, I might also see employees not thanking a customer for shopping or visiting their business when they leave. My favorite part is recording the reaction of customers after they have received poor, disappointing service or better yet, great service.

Ask Your Customers!

Unfortunately, many business owners or managers are unaware of their surroundings or rarely know what the customer is actually experiencing in their business. This information and feedback becomes extremely valuable to the business owner in evaluating what good, bad, or even ugly service their customers are receiving on a typical day. Most importantly, you will receive the feedback from the customer's perspective. After all, isn't the customer experience the most important part of the sale? I think so and I am sure your customer would agree.

What do your customers really want and are you giving it to them? Customers do not just crave good service; they crave an exceptional experience. As a business or customer service department, it is essential to find out what type of experience the customer is receiving. The simplest way to find out is to ask them.

When was the last time you evaluated your customer's experience? Disney and other top successful service companies have a plan in place to constantly evaluate their customer's experience. Here are some examples of methods that I have used as well as others to obtain valuable feedback and information from customers.

Customer Surveys and Questionnaires:

These are customer feedback methods used to gather information from customers, after they have experienced your business. Information can be obtained by phone, email, direct mail, or by a third party. The objective of this method is to ask a set of questions pertaining to their experience, value paid, willingness to return, etc.

There are two advantages with this type of feedback method. One is the ability to ask specific questions to obtain particular information from your customer. The second is the capability to ask your customer a follow-up question. A follow-up question can prove to be very valuable in receiving a true perspective of what the customer really meant when answering your first question. The challenge some businesses may have is in gathering addresses, phone numbers, and email addresses in order to send your customer the survey or questionnaire. Keep in mind that customers may or may not respond to your survey, and that obtaining the information could take time.

Customer Comment Cards:

A business can ask customers for their feedback
while they are in the middle of their experience or
before they depart. Guest Comment Cards are
usually placed on restaurant tables, checkout
counters, hotel guest rooms, lobby foyers, and even
inside your car after it has been serviced.

The advantage of this method is the ability to obtain
feedback immediately from your customers. You are
able to quickly make any necessary corrections
before future customers are affected. More
importantly you will have the capability to turn a
fair or poor customer experience around into a
positive one. You get a second-chance opportunity to
speak and empathize with the customer, correct the
problem, offer compensation if needed, and exceed
expectations for the rest of their experience, all
before they depart.

Mystery Shoppers:

This method uses an unknown third party to
experience your business as a customer. This
program is similar to parts of my Customer
Experience Makeover Coaching Program. There are
companies locally that you can contract to mystery
shop your business. Better yet, you can ask a
relative, friend, neighbor, or colleague to mystery
shop your business in return for a complimentary
gift certificate, discount, or free future visit.

Regardless of who you use, make sure they have specific scenarios or observations that you would like them to conduct and evaluate. This will help the mystery shopper obtain the specific valuable information you want. Contact me at info@johnformica.com if you would like more information on my Customer Experience Makeover Coaching Program.

Customer Focus Groups:

In this approach, you gather feedback from a random group of customers who have done business with you recently or in the past. This can be done in person, either at your business location or some other location that is convenient for your customers. It can also be conducted by phone or web telecast.

The goal is to make it convenient for your customers; this indicates your appreciation for their feedback and insight. I would also highly recommend that you include some kind of offer to the customers of the focus group to encourage them to participate.

Employee Focus Groups:

Invite key staff members who are in direct contact with the customer experience. Ask questions regarding how they perceive the customer experience, feedback they receive from customers during work, outside community perception of your business from neighbors, relatives and friends and how they believe you can make the experience better.

Many times the answers to such customer questions are right in front of you and all you have to do is ask your employees. It also can have a positive effect on the employee experience by making them feel that they are important and valued members of your business.

Managing By Walking Around

This method of obtaining feedback from customers is by far the simplest to perform, yet many take it for granted. "Managing By Walking Around"—sometimes referred to as MBWA—was a term adopted in the 80s but is still an effective method to evaluate your customer's experience.

The objective of MBWA is to inspect what you expect simply by walking around and observing and evaluating your staff, customers, policies, standards, cleanliness, operations, equipment, and anything else important in your business. When you walk around in the middle of the day, what do you see going on in your business? This can prove to be very valuable in managing your business.

MBWA can also be an effective tool in obtaining feedback from your customers by speaking to them while they are in your business, store, shop, or office, particularly during the busiest time of the business day. I suggest asking customers about their experience, value of product, and ease of doing business. Are they repeat customers or are they disappointed or frustrated?

Not only are you getting feedback firsthand from your customers, but you are in a position to help them right there on the spot. This is a great opportunity for service recovery, but more importantly you are receiving valuable feedback from your customers. Don't overlook this simple, no cost effective tool to obtain feedback from your customers in finding out what they really want.

Your goal with any of these feedback methods is to find out what your customers really want, not necessarily what they need. You then can use the information to generate higher levels of service to your customers and provide them with an exceptional customer experience, beyond just service. Customers appreciate businesses that constantly seek their feedback trying to provide a better product, service or value.

How many times have we said to ourselves as customers, "If they would only ask us how we thought we could help them with their service or product"? But we usually conclude that a particular business doesn't care what we think. Or even worse, we give the business feedback on our experience by speaking to the waiter, store clerk, or manager, only to be given the insincere "Thank you and I will let someone know about it" response. How do we feel after our conversation? The business just doesn't really care about improving their service or about what we think or want.

A customer wants to feel as if you and your business care for them as much as they care for you. When you begin to care about the customer and appreciate their feedback and concerns, you develop a deeper connection and loyalty. Then your business becomes magical!

I think the biggest challenge that small businesses have is in planning skills. Components of planning include customer service, particularly the ability to identify what is needed to be successful in their business. Small businesses need to see that this skill could vastly improve how they do business and add to their profitability.
Deborah Hardison, Small Business Director, Richmond Community College

Magical Action Plan:
Ask Your Customers

What steps can you take to get information from your customers, so that you know what they really want from their experience with your business?

Choose the two or three ways to get feedback. Then list three specific questions you will ask to get the particular feedback you want from your customers:

1._____

_____

_____

2._____

_____

_____

3._____

_____

_____

Chapter 6:
Relationships Are
Magical

What do customers really want? Customers desire a personal connection with people and organizations with whom they do business. Think about it. Why do people stop patronizing a business? What prevents them from being loyal customers? The fact is that 68% of customers who quit returning to your business do so because they don't think you, your staff, or the owners care. It may have nothing to do with price or convenience.

As a consumer, I will eventually stop giving my money to your business if I feel you don't care about me as a person or one of your loyal customers. In other words, if I feel that I am just a number and all you really care about is my money, I'll find another place down the road to give my money. I am looking for someone who cares about me and someone I might feel I have a relationship with. Do you feel the same way? I bet you would agree.

It is estimated that 50% of sales are made because of a relationship and friendship.

We all want personal attention and focus. How many of us, when we go into a restaurant, want personal attention? We want to feel welcomed and given special treatment as if we are their best customer. We go into a retail store and want a personal connection from the clerk who remembers our name and welcomes us back. If you have a financial advisor or stock broker, you want to feel as if they are personally taking care of your account even though they might also have other clients.

Let me share a great example of making a personal connection. My nephew, Michael, is a broker in New York and we like to share ideas and insight about sales, marketing, customers, and business. Michael is fairly young by most broker standards, and many times he has had to overcome the challenges of appearing young and inexperienced to his clients. However, he certainly understands the importance of relationships, particularly with his existing clients.

During the market crash of 2008, one of the first things Michael did was to call every single one of his clients to tell them that he was extremely sorry for what had happened in the market and that he felt bad for them. Michael was honest with them and said he was going to do everything in his power to help them even though he didn't have any answers at the moment, nor could he predict where the market was headed. He told them he would be discussing strategies from within his organization as well as seeking advice from many experts. Most of all, he was just calling to let them know that he understood their frustrations and again was sorry.

How many brokers do you know who did that? Mine
certainly didn't. I am not sure why. It was not his
fault that the market crashed. I don't blame him
personally. I just wondered if he was concerned. Did
he care that my 401K was now a 101K? Did he have
some kind of strategy or any insight? Unfortunately,
my wife and I did not receive much information and
had to hope it would all work out. What was our
perception? It was a very disappointing experience
for us.

Months later while the market was still crashing,
some of Michael's clients started calling him and
asking, "Michael, are you okay? How are you doing?
Are you going to make it? Are you going to stay in
business? What are you doing for money? Can I give
you a loan? What can I do to help you?" Now that is
a true example of making magic. It is all about
relationships.

Who is Caring for Grandma?

In the healthcare and medical industries, caring
relationships are extremely valuable and important
to the patient and family member. What do people
need when they go to a hospital, medical clinic,
dentist or assisted living community? We know what
they need: medical attention, lab work, a crown
filling, or a safe place where Grandma can live.

All we hope for is that somebody is going to care. Are
they going to care for me, care for my mom or dad,
my loved one, my child, or my grandparent? Just
care for them. Caring for them is what we really

want beyond the medical attention they need. We want to feel they care about our family member as much as we do. Once we believe that the staff and business cares, we become more connected to them and loyal. It is that simple. It is the secret to how you increase patient satisfaction scores.

I coach various health care businesses and professionals throughout the U.S. by helping them make the patient's healthcare experience magical. The deeper connection a healthcare facility can make with their patients and family members, the better their overall medical experience will be. We all would agree that as patients, we usually judge our experience by the way we are treated as a person, not by the way we are treated for our medical needs. Healthcare businesses that treat patients as people and empathize with them will build relationships that are magical!

Like leads to trust. Trust leads to relationships. Relationships lead to customer loyalty and buying.
Jim Cathcart

Avoiding People is Just Plain Rude!

Have you ever experienced a person being rude to you? How did you feel? What was it that the particular person did or did not do to make you feel they were being rude? You were probably being ignored in some way.

When your customers are being avoided by your employees, the perception and conclusion they form in their minds is that your staff was rude. Perhaps a customer is not greeted when walking into your business, or maybe your cashier is busy doing paper work and avoiding the opportunity to help your customer or answer questions.

Avoiding someone or being rude is the fastest way to destroy relationships. In business, it is no different. How many of your customers have felt they were ignored and thought your employees were rude? What do you think your customer's perception is of your business and first impression?

Every Person Counts

What every small business must understand is that rudeness is a personal responsibility. Each and every person who works in your business needs to be aware and personally responsible for not avoiding your customers. If just one person in your organization is rude, what is the perception of your business or organization? They're *all* rude. Is that fair? Of course not!

Have you ever visited a business, restaurant, or retail store and been ignored by an employee, waitress, or manager who passed by you without even an acknowledgement, smile, or a simple hello? It happens. But what do you tell your friends and neighbors? "Don't go there. Service is terrible!" You form a perception and conclusion from just one employee, waiter, or waitress. Your perception of the entire business or restaurant now becomes one of disappointment. The business probably is not that bad, but it is too late to get you back as a customer.

Every person counts in your company, even those employees who only work in the back of the house area of your business. I promise you, it can take just one time to make a lasting negative impression. What if one of your employees steps out into the reception area where customers are present and avoids acknowledging them or saying a simple hello? What will your customers or clients think? Your employees are all rude and their perception of your business is not a positive one. Can you afford that perception and possible loss of customers in today's tough business world?

Overwhelm Your Customers with Kindness

One of the many things we did at Disney's Yacht and Beach Club Resort to create a great customer experience—as well as customer loyalty—was to focus on eliminating avoidance. Have you ever stayed at a four or five star hotel that provided a bellman to assist you with your luggage upon arrival or at checkout? In any typical hotel lobby, you will find a bell captain's desk with bellmen standing around the desk, waiting to assist guests with their luggage.

I never cared for that strategy, so I wanted to do something different and unique to create a great customer experience for our guests. I discussed the situation with my bell staff and we came up with a new strategy that was more customer-friendly. Each bellman was placed strategically around the lobby except for one bellman who would occupy the bell captain's desk and answer the phone. The others were scattered around the lobby of the hotel at strategic points where they could have a biggest impact on our guests. Bellman were stationed by the elevators, the doors leading out to the swimming pool, near the restaurant entrance, and by the exit doors where guest would walk out to catch the buses to take them to the various parks.

Every bellman had a role. When guests would come off the elevator, the bellman would greet them with a friendly "Good morning!" or "Hello, how are you today?" "Hey, nice hat! Are you a big Braves fan? How are the Braves going to do today?" The bellman might strike up a conversation and ask, "What are your plans today?" If the guests were going to the Magic Kingdom park, the bellman might reply, "When you enter the park, make sure that you ask where the characters are signing autographs today. It is a great experience for the kids."

The bellman next to the restaurant would greet guest with a friendly good morning and might recommend today's special "Mickey Mouse" pancakes. The bellman stationed at the front entrance doors would greet and say goodbye to guests, share unique park information or suggest taking an umbrella because it's probably going to rain today. Guests going out to the pool would be acknowledged by the bellman stationed by the doors reminding the guests to use suntan lotion to protect them from the hot Florida sun.

Do you know what response I received from the guests staying at the hotel? "What on earth are you feeding your employees? They're killing us with kindness! Everywhere we go, your people are so friendly and helpful."

Our goal was to create a perception that everybody is friendly, cheerful, and going out of their way to provide a great experience. It worked. In fact it worked so well that Disney's Yacht and Beach Club Hotel received the highest guest satisfaction ratings among all Disney Resort Hotels. When asked on a survey "Would you stay at this resort hotel on your next visit?" the results were overwhelmingly positive.

Shortly after, I was approached by the Disney Institute, a professional development division of the Walt Disney World organization and asked how we obtained such high scores. Later the Disney Institute used my insight for the development of a new seminar called "Customer Loyalty". Disney's Yacht and Beach Club Resort Hotel, as well as my staff, were used as a model for the program. I was also asked to facilitate a portion of the program and share it to business professionals around the world. The seminar became a huge success.

All businesses would love to know how to create and build customer loyalty. I am not sure that there is a better example of customer loyalty than what the Disney organization and Disney brand has created and maintains today.

How much do you think it cost my department to
"kill people with kindness"? Not a dime! We didn't
need a budget increase or to sacrifice service
somewhere else. All we had to do is make sure we
never avoided our guests. It was our choice to make
our relationships with our guests magical. We called
it the "10 foot radius" rule. Acknowledge and greet
everyone— including fellow employees—if you are
within 10 feet of them. Try it in your business or
organization. It will certainly create a magical
experience for all.

Customers Remember Courteous People Over Efficient Service

How many of you would agree that when you visit
Walt Disney World and travel around the parks,
resorts and entertainment centers that it is amazing
how efficient they are in getting you and your family
around? Hundreds of thousands of visitors coming
into Walt Disney World throughout the day, yet
somehow the Disney organization seems to
effortlessly make it all happen.

Walt Disney World Resort does a remarkable job by
being so efficient. But is that what we all remember
and talk about to our friends and relatives when we
return home? Mostly we comment on how friendly,
helpful and courteous all the staff was during our
visit. We talk about how cheerful and excited the
staff was in serving us. Being efficient is certainly
important in the customer experience, but being
courteous, helpful, friendly, cheerful and

enthusiastic to serve is what customers remember most about their experience.

Quite honestly, I have found that most leaders, business managers, CEOs, presidents, and bosses, place their focus and importance of the business, employees and customer experience on being efficient. Businesses spend much of their time on efficiency, tasks and outcomes. I am all for that, but not if you sacrifice being courteous or truly caring for your customer's well being and experience.

If being efficient is more important in your business you will miss out on opportunities and experiences that your customers will really remember about your business and talk about. Just like at Walt Disney World, customers remember people over product. Is the purpose more important than the job? In most businesses, I would bet, caring and serving others and being courteous has a bigger impact on the customer experience over tasks, outcomes, and just being efficient.

Customers are not loyal to a business, restaurant, printer, grocery store, hotel chain, office supply, gas station or financial advisor. They are usually loyal to the relationship that is created from their experience.

Magical Action Plan: Make Relationships Magical

Here are some tips to make magic moments for your customers:

- Be *interested* in your customer, not interesting.
- Be *first* to say hello with a contagious positive attitude and excitement to serve.
- *Smile,* and be *cheerful* to create a friendly atmosphere.
- Acknowledge every customer within *a 10 foot radius* to avoid a perception of avoiding or rudeness.
- Make an extra effort to remember and use people's *names.*
- Make everyone *feel important* as if they are the only person in the room, including their children.
- Show others that you are *enjoying* the conversation with them.
- Display *positive* body language.
- Listen, listen, *listen!*
- Don't *interrupt* people.
- *Compliment* others about what they are wearing, doing, and saying.
- Thank them all the time by saying *"Thank you!"*

Chapter 7:
Always on Stage: The Magic is in the Details

Have you've ever been inside a Walt Disney World park or hotel and noticed the cleanliness and the attention that is placed upon all those little details? The areas are usually clean and free from litter, windows are smudge-free, flowers and plants are manicured to perfection, music is themed, and everything seems to be in its proper place. At Disney, the attention to details matters. Why does Disney go through great lengths to pay attention to the details?

Disney calls it "being on stage". For example, when a movie picture is being made and filmed, a movie producer goes to great lengths to make sure the exact stage, scenery, lighting, outside sounds, and costumes are in place. You would agree that all of these details matter in order to produce and create the effects of a successful movie. Disney uses that same philosophy with their parks and hotels.

First Impressions - Magical Moments of Truth

Do you think first impressions are important? I like to call them your magical moments of truth. Let's

look at it from the customer's viewpoint. In just
seven seconds or less, a person forms ten or more
impressions of you, your organization, business or
the service you are about to provide. What do your
customers experience in the first seven seconds as
they enter your business? What do they see, hear,
and perhaps even smell?

Focus on your people. Are they helpful, courteous, do
they avoid people? Is everyone wearing uniforms?
What does their appearance look like? Are they
knowledgeable and confident when asked a
question? Are they professional?

When was the last time you took a closer look at
your store front or business entrance? Look at it as if
you were about to host the President of the United
States, a popular movie star, the mayor of your city,
or some other VIP. Do you have entrance signs that
are crooked? What do your parking lot, storefront
windows, doors, and sidewalks look like? Do you
have scotch tape holding faded pieces of paper on
windows and doors? Are there cigarette butts
cluttered around the sidewalk in front of your doors?
Do you have fingerprints on windows? These are all
first impressions and moments of truth that your
customers experience each and every day.

One of the many leadership positions that I held at
the Walt Disney World Resort in Orlando was the
Executive Housekeeping Manager at Disney's Grand
Floridian Beach Resort. This hotel is Disney's
flagship five-star property and my role was to make
sure that it always looked that way. Inside the hotel,

there was brass everywhere. I had two employees
working full time, seven days a week cleaning and
polishing brass railings, brass stairways, brass
doors, signs, and fixtures all throughout the hotel. A
dull finish and fingerprints on brass were not
acceptable for our guests. Why? It was a choice. Was
there a cost? Absolutely!

If you want to make a magical, once-in-a-lifetime
first impression to people when they walk into the
immaculate, Victorian-themed, five-star hotel, you
must choose to make it happen. The result is what
people say when they enter and walk into the lobby.
"Wow! Unbelievable! Spectacular! This place is just
gorgeous!" That is the experience that Disney is
trying to create each time, every day of the year.

So why would any small business, not necessary a
five star hotel, accept and allow a sub-standard
appearance to exist in their business? The simple
answer is that it is nothing more than a choice. In
my 30-plus years of experience, I have heard every
excuse in the book:

- "We are short-staffed."
- Too busy
- Cut-backs on staff
- Saving money
- Poorly performing employees
- Bad outside contractors
- "I thought someone else was going to do it."

While all of these excuses are piling up, what are
your customers experiencing each and every day,

minute by minute, second by second while visiting
your business? How many customers have been lost
by-passing a business because it did not appear to be
pleasant, clean, appealing, or even safe? Would you
be impressed with their lack of attention to details?
Of course not, and neither would others. For any
small business, it is nothing more than making a
choice.

Every small business should look at the details and
first impressions of their business as if they were
filming a movie. What on-stage viewpoint are your
customers experiencing every day?

Your Employees Are Actors in a Show

In a Broadway show, the appearance of the actors
and actresses also plays an important part of the
show. In your business, the appearance of your
employees is just as important. In fact, the
appearance of your employees makes up 55% of the
message that leads your customers to form an
impression about your business. Consider your
employees as being on stage and performing a show
for each and every customer.

How do your employees look at work, and what
message and impressions are you creating in your
business or office from their appearance? Are you
satisfied with how they look? Do you think your
customers even notice? They do, and they are
forming an opinion of your business, just as they
would with actors and actresses in a movie or
Broadway show.

Disney employees are known for their clean-cut no-nonsense appearance. Again, it is all part of being on stage. In fact, there are Generals and CEOs of many companies that would not be allowed to work for Disney because of the company's strict standards for appearance and grooming. These guidelines are very specific and spelled out in numerous pages in their employee handbook.

Examples of grooming standards for male employees include no mustaches or other facial hair, no long sideburns, no long hair, no earrings, no visible body piercings, no excessive jewelry, no extreme hair color, and no visible tattoos. Grooming guideline examples for females include only one earring per ear, certain makeup, lipstick, no extreme hair color, no excessive jewelry, and no brightly-colored fingernail polish or very long fingernails, and no visible tattoos.

Why does Disney go to great lengths to make sure all of their employees look this way? Do male employees perform better without mustaches, long hair or earrings? Do female employees serve customers better if their makeup or fingernails are a certain color? I don't believe so. However, it is all part of the show. Disney's goal is to create a clean, wholesome, and family-friendly image for their parks and resorts, and the appearance of their employees is a big part of the customer experience.

Does the appearance of your employees become a part of your customer experience and moment of truth? Does it matter? It should, and certainly

matters to your customers and their comfort level in
possibly doing business with you.

Don't Scare Your Customers Away

I once coached an assisted living community that
had many operational challenges. My objective was
to help them correct high staff turnover, poor
service, numerous violations, lack of consistency, low
resident count, and an unfavorable reputation in the
community. It certainly was a challenge.

One of the very first issues we wanted to address
was grooming guidelines. The existing staff had no
guidelines, as far as I knew. The appearance of the
caregivers consisted of extremely long fingernails,
strange hair styles, nose and eyebrow piercing, and
an overall lack of professionalism.

Since it was obvious that the customers in the home
were mostly elderly people, what atmosphere and
impression was created by the appearance of the
staff? Do you think the elderly customers liked it?
Do you think perhaps that some of them might have
been a little uncomfortable looking at employees
with nose and eyebrow piercings? It probably was
not the best atmosphere or impression that could
have been created.

We wrote up new specific grooming guidelines,
similar to—but not exactly the same as—Disney's to
create an atmosphere where the residents would be
more comfortable. We immediately received some
interesting feedback from the staff. "I can't believe

this. What are you trying to do, turn this place into Disney World?" Of course that was not our intent. However, the organization and staff needed to understand the mindset of the customers and create a friendly atmosphere and experience to match.

Some of the staff understood and caught on; others who did not made new employment choices instead. If we were going to turn things around in that assisted living community, we had to get everyone onboard. The staff needed to make a commitment and show that they really cared by making the residents feel comfortable in their own community home.

We created the new grooming guidelines based specifically for the customers, not for the benefit of the staff. It worked, along with the many other changes that needed to made, to improve the overall customer experience.

Does your business or organization have what is frequently called "Casual or Dress Down Fridays"? I must tell you that I am not a big fan of such programs. Why do businesses have "Casual Fridays"? Usually, when asked, their response is, "It boosts morale and productivity. My employees love it and their attitudes around the office on Fridays are great!" What this tells me is your employees are wonderful on Fridays but are they are allowed to be jerks, with bad attitudes, Saturdays through Thursdays? Are your customers any different on Fridays? Should they receive better service only on Fridays? Of course not, but your grooming guidelines are then based on your employee wants rather than what your customers really want.

Think about how your customer experience might be compromised by a "Casual Friday" day. If your moments of truth and first impression are to have a professional environment, what will your customers think if everyone in your business is wearing golf shirts and jeans? Is that the first impression you want to make? The choice is yours.

How many businesses do you know that lower the standard of appearance because they can't find or hire enough staff? Disney doesn't lower their grooming guidelines in order to staff their parks and resorts. In fact, Disney uses its grooming guidelines as a screening method when hiring potential candidates.

I saw this firsthand one day while helping out in their "Casting Center" (Hiring Center). In the beginning process, applicants watch a short video on Disney's grooming guidelines and strict standards before completing their applications. After the video, I observed potential candidates walking out and not bothering to complete the rest of the process.

I am sure some of them did not agree with the standards and didn't want to conform to the strict grooming guidelines. It was certainly their right and choice, but that is exactly what Disney wanted. Disney is looking for people who believe in what they believe in and who buy into their culture and philosophy.

I am not advocating that your business implement strict grooming guidelines the way Disney does. However, your grooming and appearance guidelines should be based on your customer expectations, not employee satisfaction. Whatever image or first impression you are trying to create, make sure you consider the mindset of your customers. Their first impressions of your business are forming in just seven seconds or less. Make sure those first impressions are creating a magical experience for your customers.

Paying attention to all of the details is only a matter of choice. If Disney and other successful businesses choose to do it, and it creates a positive customer experience, why can't any small business choose to do it as well? The answer is that they can. Any business or organization—large or small, family-run, new business or existing business—can do it. They just have to choose to do it. What will your business choose to do?

Magical Action Plan: Make First Impressions Magical

Evaluate the first impressions that your customers get when they first make contact and or walk into your business or organization? Look at the surroundings, signage, parking lot, front doors and entranceways. Look around the lobby, reception area or hostess desk. Don't forget to also focus on people. Are people distracted by computers and task work rather than greeting customers, asking questions or being helpful as your customers enter your business?

After evaluating and listing these first impressions, ask yourself and the staff this question: Which impressions would we want to be remembered by? What do we want our customers, when they leave after doing business with us, to remember? Customers remember those first impressions. Make sure you and your business pay attention to the details, even the small ones. Hint: Don't forget to take the taped pieces of paper off your windows and doors.

Chapter 8:
Everyone Can Make Magic

I was once shopping in one of those big box office supply stores while a cashier was faced with a customer who wanted to exchange his mechanical pencil for another pencil. The cashier responded with a typical reply, "Do you have a receipt?" The customer did not have a receipt and the cashier said, "I am sorry, we can't do a refund or exchange without a receipt." Sound familiar?

Obviously the customer wasn't happy, and wanted to speak with a manager. A manager arrived shortly to handle the situation. He asked the customer again if he had a receipt. The customer at this point began to elevate his frustrations at the manager. The manager sensed this and said, "You know what, sir? I'll let you go back and get another one if you like. Sorry for the inconvenience."

Let me ask you a question. Did it take 25 years of management experience to make that decision? Do you need a college degree? Why couldn't the hourly employee make that same decision? Guess how much the pencil cost? Sixty nine cents! How do you think the poor cashier felt after her manager stepped in and made that decision? Do you think the employee felt important or valued? Do you think the employee was given the opportunity to provide great customer service? After all, isn't that what she gets paid to do?

The Answer Is Yes! Now, What Was the Question?

One of the biggest reasons why businesses fail in creating a magical customer experience is they do not allow their employees the opportunity to make magic. Here is where most magical experience opportunities are lost.

I believe that most employees, if you hire the right ones, want to do a great job. If given the chance and if they believe in what you believe: great customer service. Employees get enjoyment out of helping and serving others. They want to make people happy, or satisfy a disappointed customer by providing a refund and doing whatever they can to make it right for the customer.

Your employees certainly know why the customer is frustrated or upset. However, the problem usually is that the employees are not given a chance to serve the customer and provide a magical experience. This is mostly because of the authoritarian, top-down, "management makes all the decisions" philosophy that many businesses have created. Does this sound familiar? "Sorry, I have to go ask my manager." Or "Oh I am sorry; company policy says... so we can't do that! I would like to help you, but..."

Remove the "But" & Take Off the Handcuffs

As the Disney organization evolved over time, it realized that a management-controlling environment would not provide a great customer experience. It then began to eliminate all the middle bureaucracy and empower the staff to make more decisions. Disney's goal was to place the decision making and problem solving closer to the people who have direct contact with customers. especially when it came to dealing with customer complaints or the opportunity to create a special experience for their guests.

The results of the new initiative were extremely positive and effective. The staff felt more important and valued. Think about your business. What bureaucracy can you eliminate? Just get rid of it. Begin putting some responsibility in the hands of the employees to make the decisions. Your employees are on the front lines. Give them the opportunity, train them, teach them, provide them guidelines, but then let them make decisions that create a good or better customer experience. As long as it is in the best interest of the customer, what else matters?

If you are concerned that your staff will make poor decisions, provide a coaching opportunity. "Was the customer satisfied with your decision? Great! Can you think of any other options that would have been just as effective and satisfying to the customer? What might we do differently next time?" That is what coaching and leadership are all about. It's not about controlling or scolding your people over their decisions. "You should have done this, or you could have done that". These types of statements do not create a valued or positive work environment. The situation is over. That the customer went away happy is all that matters. Any business should be thankful it has an employee that at least cares about its customers.

The sad fact is that this particular office scenario—and others similar to it—go on every day in our business world. Most managers and business owners don't even realize it. Why? Because they get hung up on believing that only managers or supervisors are capable of making decisions. I actually asked the manager in the office store example why he—not his employee—had to make that decision. His response to me was, "Oh, if I let my employees give away things to our customers the next thing they might do is give away laptops, desks, and software."

"Really?" I said. "Maybe you hired the wrong people, especially if you don't trust them." He shrugged his shoulders and said, "Maybe, but it is so hard to find good people that want to work." How pathetic that statement was. In fact when I asked the cashier how she felt after the incident, she told me she didn't understand why she could not make that same decision. She enjoyed making customers happy but was not trusted to do so. Perhaps the manager did hire the right person. Unfortunately, the problem is with the manager who literally had put the employee in handcuffs.

Take a good look at your policies and rules regarding
compensating customers, giving refunds or
exchanges. Ask yourself "How would I feel if I were
in the customer's shoes?" Focus on the customer's
point of view. Train and coach your employees to
make good decisions in the best interest of your
customers. Take the handcuffs off your employees by
allowing them the opportunity to take good care of
your customers. "The answer is yes, now what is the
question?"

Magical Action Plan: Empower Your Employees to Make Magic

You can change the culture and environment of how your customers get treated. Here is where you can make real magic!

1. Review all the policies that might affect a customer experience in your business.
2. Make a list, and as a group, evaluate each one.
3. One at a time, tackle, change, or eliminate each policy that ties the hands of your staff or might provide a negative experience for your customers.
4. Ask your staff for their input and suggestions and come up with alternative solutions.

You don't have to change everything at once. Start with the most important ones that frustrate your customers or staff. Put yourself in your customer's shoes and focus on their point of view.

Chapter 9:
Whistle While
You Work

*Fun boils down to one word: energy. Substitute the
word "energy" for "fun" and then ask yourself, "Do I
want more or less energy when I am working?*
Clifford Kuhn, "The Fun Factor"

Have you ever noticed when visiting Disney World
that the employees seem to be happy and having fun
at what they do? They always appear to be friendly,
smiling, full of energy, and—most of all—having a
good time doing what they do. At Disney, we had a
motto. "Work hard but have fun and play hard." Are
your employees appearing the same way? Are they
enjoying what they do and having fun at work? If
not, do you know why?

Many small business owners and leaders generally
agree that humor and having fun is something good
to encourage in the workplace. They will agree that
people who enjoy doing what they do, with a sense of
humor, are probably better at their jobs. However,
when thinking of having fun in the workplace, many
business leaders have a misconception that fun and
humor encourage irresponsible behavior.

Numerous concerned business owners have asked me, "If I support and encourage fun and humor in the workplace, wouldn't that send the wrong message?" They fear that their people will become distracted from the serious responsibilities and tasks that must be performed, and their business might lose its competitive edge. Many also fear that managers and supervisors will lose respect for their authority and control. I can understand how they might feel.

However, let's think about this. Aren't we all more productive when we are doing something that is fun and enjoyable? Anything that is done at a level of excellence or in pursuit of excellence is usually exciting and fun. The Disney organization is a great example of this in their pursuit of excellence.

Why should you use humor and fun in your business? It is simple. By making an effort to include and maintain a fun work environment you will make your business more successful and magical. What do I mean by being successful and magical? Success and magic in your business come down to one indispensible factor, and that is satisfied customers. You cannot survive and be successful without satisfied and happy customers. Happy employees are the best guarantee for happy customers.

Benefits of Having Fun in the Workplace

Create an atmosphere for fun in the workplace and you'll get great work. When a workplace atmosphere is fun, employees will want to come to work. Morale goes up, absenteeism decreases, performance and productivity will improve. Employees will gain greater satisfaction from their work, and turnover in your business will go down.

Tasks that are done at a level of excellence are fun and exciting. Tasks that are done at a level of poor or average are boring, monotonous, and just a plain drag. When you are having fun at work, it doesn't feel like work does it?

So why don't businesses create and implement more fun and humor in the workplace? That is a good question. We all have seen that employees who enjoy what they are doing and are having fun are certainly better at customer service, particularly in providing a better customer experience. Here are a few of the benefits of a fun working environment.

Free Advertising

Have you ever flown on Southwest Airlines? It is quite an experience, isn't it? What do we talk about the most? Probably all the fun the staff is having. When the flight attendants and customer service agents are using humor, playing games, and creating fun with the customers, it is like free advertising. We all talk about the experience to our friends and coworkers.

As I travel around the U.S., I often hear wonderful stories about songs, games, and skits that were told during flight delays. Humor starts at the top and flows across the entire Southwest business culture.

It is practiced on the ground, in the sky, at the gates and even in the commercials that they make.

I always look forward to seeing Southwest Airline commercials on TV. In one particular commercial, I enjoyed seeing their baggage handlers lifting their shirts up to display their message written on their exposed bellies, that "bags fly free". The handlers certainly looked like they were having fun. I would think handling heavy luggage and bags all day isn't exactly fun, but who wouldn't want to work with them after seeing the commercial?

As a customer, what is your perception of a baggage handler at Southwest? If the baggage handlers are having fun, I can just imagine what the rest of my experience with the other employees will be. I look forward to my flight and can't wait to experience one of those crazy, fun, Southwest airline experiences myself and share with my friends. Isn't that free advertising?

How many of you have been to Disney World or Disneyland and have had a great personal experience from a Disney cast member and couldn't wait to tell someone? When your customers talk about their fun and pleasant experiences, it becomes free advertising.

Fun Breeds More Energy and a Healthier Workforce

How many of us have more energy when playing a recreational sport or working on a hobby we enjoy?

We seem to be able to play golf, softball or tennis for hours and hours in the summer heat but complain to our bosses about not being able to work when the air conditioning system isn't working properly. Why?

Why do people have more energy doing recreational activities than they do at work? Because playing those recreational activities is more fun! Making sure that there is more fun in your workplace is a way to make sure that there is more energy.

The truth is that fun at work makes us better and healthier at work. There is documented proof that having fun reduces stress, boosts immunity, relieves pain, decreases anxiety, prevents depression, rests the brain, enhances communication, inspires creativity, maintains hope, and boost morale. Research also shows that when we are having fun and laughing, we produce endorphins, our bodies' natural life-giving healing medicine. So when work is fun and employees are free to have fun, laugh and play, people are healthier.

There is truth behind the saying, "Fun and laughter are the best medicine". If people are healthier, unwanted absenteeism becomes extinct. People want to come to work when they are having fun. Why wouldn't you or your employees want all those benefits in your business?

Having Fun Breeds Success

Do you remember the late Steve Irwin, better known as "The Crocodile Hunter"? He loved what he did and was really good at it. Steve blew people away and it wasn't just about animals. No matter the subject, he was interested, inquisitive, excited, and got all that he could out of every experience in life.

Do you know the difference between Steve Irwin and most of us? Two things. First, he loved what he did. His fame and wealth came out of his passion for his career. Second, no matter what he was doing, he kept asking, "What's interesting about this?" "How do they do that?" "How can I make this more fun?" "How can we do it better or more efficiently?" "What can we do to make this job less boring?"

Having fun first is what leads to success, not the other way around. If we lack fun to concentrate exclusively on success we will miss a great opportunity in achieving success in business as well as in our individual jobs.

Ask yourself these questions:

- Where did you first get the idea that you wanted to do the work you have chosen?
- Who influenced you?
- Why do you think this line of work would be good for you?
- How do you define success?
- Do you have a purpose?

These are all important questions that will define your environment at work. The environment you choose will set the tone for your team, business, and employees. It will also create a positive, enjoyable atmosphere and experience for your customers.

Southwest Airlines continues to make a profit year after year, even though they are known to have the smallest number of employees per aircraft and serve the most customers per employee. The people at Southwest Airlines are passionate about the pursuit of having fun.

Successful companies like Southwest, Disney, and Starbucks have all created a business environment and culture that has inspired creativity, innovativeness, problem solving, passion, dedication, unselfishness, teamwork and ownership. I truly believe that you can make a strong case that those are the result of having fun.

Having Fun Makes Magic

Your employees will more likely go out of their way to help and serve customers if they are having fun. Who wouldn't want to make people happy at Disney World? It would sure be fun, don't you think?

At Disney, I knew my housekeeping staff. In the midst of a sometimes difficult and exhausting job cleaning sixteen or more guest rooms a day, they were having fun. They truly enjoyed tucking and placing children's dolls and stuffed animals under the covers as if they were sleeping while the family was at the park. Some housekeepers created small scenes with them having tea, looking out the window or watching TV.

It was amazing to watch and witness their creativity. As their manager, do you think I told them that they had to do it? Never! They did it because they were allowed to have fun, and they wanted to do it because it was fun to do. It certainly made people happy.

My staff would go out of their way celebrating anniversaries, guests' birthdays, and special occasions by having fun and doing fun things for our guests. I had front desk clerks go home and purchase—on their own—a certain toy for a child to replace one that had been broken during their travels to Disney World from their home town. It was no fun to see a sad or disappointed child in the resort. It was much more fun to see the child's face when the new toy arrived. How do you think the parents felt and reacted? They were certainly surprised, thrilled and very grateful. Now that's magical!

We had maintenance workers who took pride in learning—on their own—as much as they could about the different parks, hours of operation, best place to see the parade, where you could find Mickey, getting to and from the hotels, and more. Why? They were often approached by puzzled guests with questions throughout the hotel and it was fun to answer their questions, provide helpful insights, feel valued, and of course make people happy. Fun certainly breeds energy and excitement in a job.

We often spend much of our time focusing on all of the negatives and problems in our businesses.

Although important, there is not much fun in it. This is particularly true for our front line employees who need to focus on creating a positive experience for our customers. If you focus on what you can do for the customer to make their experience better, I will assure you it will be more fun for your employees. Give them the opportunity and you will find that their fun and enjoyable actions will put you ahead of your competition, and most of all, create customer loyalty. It doesn't have to cost your business lots of money to do it.

Remember the little things and attention to details that matter most. Write a thank-you note, or phone call, acknowledge a special anniversary or birthday, have fun with your customer's children, give samples of a new dinner entrée or appetizer, or make your customers feel special. All of those matter and are fun to do.

Isn't that why you are in business in the first place?

Make sure all of your employees know that and feel the same way. Most of all, give them the opportunity to make magic. They will have fun doing it: maybe even more than your customers experiencing it. Fun will make you successful and your business successful.

I could go on and on telling you all the wonderful stories and magic that my employees at Disney and other companies created for visiting guests and customers. I am sure you also have some wonderful stories. In fact, if you have an example from a

business, store, restaurant, or employee who left you
with a magical experience, I would love to hear
about it.

Please send the example or stories to me on my web
site at <u>www.johnformica.com</u>. I will be compiling all
of the examples and will be delighted to share some
of them on my weekly "Magical Moment Minute". I
know these examples will inspire others with new
ideas to make magic in their own businesses and
organizations. Feel free to sign up at any time. It's
free!

If You're Not Having Fun, Do Something Else

Do you enjoy your job? What do you really love about
what you are doing right now? What could you do to
love your job more? If there is nothing that you enjoy
about your business or job or what you are doing,
you need to think about quitting. What? I am not
saying to go out and close the doors of your business
or tell your boss that you quit, but you might think
hard about considering it in the very near future.

If you do not enjoy what you do, then you are
probably not very good at it. If you are not any good
at it, then you are probably not one of the most liked
members of your team or at work. When you go
home from work being miserable, you probably do
nothing but gripe and complain, which is not fair to
your family.

An absence of enjoyment indicates a presence of
frustration and dissatisfaction. Dissatisfaction and

frustration leads to negativity which can impact the customer experience. Customers have no problem identifying a negative business environment. The attitudes of employees who whine and complain certainly creep into coworkers, service, and more importantly, your customers. In the workplace you need to focus on finding ways to create more fun at work to overcome those negative "stinking thinking" people who make work days miserable.

Again, think of the example of the late Steve Irwin, The Crocodile Hunter". He certainly loved his job and had a passion for what he did in his career. You can too!

Circumstances can either make us or break us. The choice is ours.
Zig Ziglar

How can you make today more fun? How can you make your work easier today, while actually maintaining top quality, customer focus, and high efficiency? Keep asking those questions and more like them, and share them with your coworkers. Stop whining and complaining and do something about it. Dr. Wayne Dyer says it best: "There is no scarcity of opportunity to make a living at what you love. There is only scarcity of resolve to make it happen."

So try today to find something good or purposeful in what you do at work and begin to create a "whistle while you work" atmosphere at your company, for your team and even at home. I promise you that your boss, customers, coworkers and family will all appreciate it.

Ten Tips to Make the Workplace Fun and Magical

Smile first thing every morning and get it over with!
W.C. Fields

Let's look at some ways to make the workplace fun.

1. **Smile More:** Never underestimate the power of a smile. Keep your focus on smiling no matter what you are called upon to do. It will create a cheerful and friendly atmosphere for your coworkers and customers. The best part of smiling is that it doesn't cost anything to smile.

2. **Think Fun All the Time:** Try and focus on fun and positive thoughts. Image or visualize good outcomes. Be optimistic and stay away from negative people who are pessimistic and will bring you down.

3. **Laugh at Yourself:** It is not a form of humiliation. Appreciate that we are not perfect. Take *your* work seriously but not yourself. Laugh with others and not at others. Laugh with and at what people do or what you do and never at others because of who they are.

4. **Focus on Success:** Start a Success Journal in your business. Write down one great thing, conversation, accomplishments or positive experience about your business or day. Keep the journal out so others can see it. Post customer

testimonials everywhere and around the business and discuss them at meetings.

5. **Let Go of the Baggage:** Houseclean all of your small irritations and previous bad experiences. Taking resentments and grudges into the workplace will bog you down, and stifle productivity, creativity and fun.

6. **Designate a No Complaining Day:** Try and see if you and your staff can go an entire day at work and not complain. If a person has a complaint they must bring it to their manager along with at least one or two solutions to the problem, obstacle or opportunity. Extend it to a week or month if you can.

7. **Keep Things Fresh:** Avoid business as usual. Do things differently by cross training employees in different jobs, tasks and even responsibilities. Break up your routines at work. Redecorate your office, business lobby or storefront. You will become more creative and innovative with your customers.

8. **Play and Make it a Game:** This is a great way to put fun in any activity, task or chore. Taking the time to do this will make it fun and go faster. Reward yourself and team when you reached your goal.

9. **Don't Accept Sloppy Work**: When you accept sloppy work, poor service, dirty restrooms, carpets, windows, desks, rudeness and behavior, what will you get in your business? All of the above. Don't let the sloppy work become the norm in your business.

10. **Celebrate Everything:** Constant celebrations breed joy. Acknowledge your employees, managers, customers and clients. Make a big

deal out of little successes along the way. It will make people feel important, valued and appreciated. It will surely be fun and magical!

People treat their customers the same way they get treated.

Magical Action Plan: Make the Workplace Fun and Magical

Sit down with your staff and list things that will make the job, tasks or environment more fun in your business or workplace. Keep it simple. Challenge each other to come up with things that do not cost any money or serious change in business. And of course, make the process fun!

_____

_____

_____

_____

_____

_____

_____

_____

The Magical Conclusion: Dream, Dare, Believe, and Do!

Dream of all the success you can have in your small business or organization. If you could run your business like Disney, what would it look like? Visualize your employees having fun and providing a great and magical experience to your customers. Dream big! Share your dreams with your employees and get everyone excited about the possibilities of success. Keep the dream alive. Martin Luther King didn't say "I have a plan" or "I have a new idea". He said with passion and conviction: "I have a dream." What is your dream for your business? Where do you see your business a year, two years, five years, or ten years from now? Do you have a purpose or just a mission statement?

Dare yourself, team, or employees to do things differently. If your business is not where you want it to be, what are you going to do differently? If your customers are not happy or you are constantly trying to find new customers because your existing customers aren't coming back, what are you going to do about it? I dare you to do things differently. I dare you to look at needs to change and actually put these strategies and proven success principle in your daily small business practice. While you were reading this book, what was going on back in your business? Do you think there is a better or easier way to make magic in your business? Are you looking for the opportunity to buy some "pixie dust"? No one said it would be easy, but I dare you and your team to try. I dare you!

Believe in your purpose, your business, your team, your employees, and even yourself. You can do this. You can make the needed and necessary changes to make your business magical. Believe that you can create a magical, positive environment and atmosphere for your customers and staff. If you are a business owner or manager reading this book and aren't excited and believe in making changes, why did you read it? If you don't believe you can improve your customer experience, or work environment, if you don't believe that you can make your customers happy, create customer loyalty, and increase profits or serve others, then what makes you think your employees will believe it either?

Find and hire people who believe in what you believe in and they will go through brick walls for you and your customers. You are the thermostat in your business. Are you hot or cold? Are you a pessimist or an optimist? Do you dread coming to work each day? Do you passionately believe in your purpose?

I believe in you. I believe in your entrepreneur spirit where small businesses and their success is the foundation for our success as a country. We as a country can no longer depend on large companies to employ our families and friends. The engines of our economy are run by small businesses like yours. I believe you can do it!

Do it! Success is 90% perspiration and 10% technique. Roll up your sleeves and get to work. Start small and try one success principle at a time that you learned from this book. If you try to incorporate everything from this book it will seem to be overwhelming, a chore and of course not fun. What will stop you? Are you too busy with not enough time? Choose to make the time, one magical strategy at a time.

Are you worried that your employees won't like the new changes that you feel are needed in order to create a magical experience? My answer to that is to share your excitement and enthusiasm with them, give them the opportunity and have fun doing it. If you have employees who do not want to work towards your purpose and take great care of your customers then go out and find new employees who believe in what you believe. What is going to stop you? I hope nothing. Go out and do it! Make some magic! Your business, employees, customers, and community will love you for it.

Don't only give the customer what they expect. Give your customer an experience they will always remember. It will surely be 'Magical'.

GO MAKE SOME MAGIC!

About the Author

John Formica (an "Ex-Disney Guy") is a nationally known speaker and "America's Best Customer Experience Coach". He is also President of John Formica Enterprises, LLC, a training and team coaching firm specializing in leadership development, personal and employee performance, team relationships, business growth, and enhancing the customer experience. John has partnered with numerous industries, including health care, manufacturing, retail, restaurants, hotels, colleges, school districts, governmental and non-profit agencies, and business professionals around the U.S.

Prior to becoming a professional speaker and customer experience coach, John held numerous top management positions with service industry leaders including Walt Disney World Resorts, Hyatt Hotels, Hilton Hotels and Sunrise Senior Living Inc. John's leadership and passion for customer service influenced Team accomplishments including the Zagat award for the Top 10 Resort Hotel in the U.S. and Pinnacle Award Winner for one of the Best Convention Hotels in North Carolina, as well as successfully improving resident care satisfaction scores as an Executive Director with Sunrise Senior Living.

During his 10 years at the Walt Disney World Resort in Orlando, Florida, John was a manager in the Rooms Division of their top two luxury resort properties: Disney's Grand Floridian Beach Resort and Disney's Yacht and Beach Club Resort. There John successfully led his teams to achieve the highest guest satisfaction ratings among all Disney World Resort Hotels. John also was selected to co-chair the company rollout of "Disney's Guest Satisfaction Program" as well as deliver presentations for the Disney Institute on "Customer Loyalty" to companies and business professionals all over the world.

John's 25 years as a professional leader with the Walt Disney World Resort organization and other top service industries, bring a wealth of knowledge and practical, not theory, hands-on, high energy, experience to his team coaching, training seminars, and keynote presentations. He has delivered more than 1,450 presentations to industries, conferences, and business professionals, while earning a reputation for being enthusiastic, creative, practical, and highly motivating. John's many articles are in demand and appear in a number of industry publications and business journals.

John has also thrilled and inspired conferences and audiences to overcome challenges and reach for success in business and in life by sharing his incredible, life changing adventure to the summit of Mount Rainier.

JOHN FORMICA

(an "Ex-Disney Guy")
America's Best Customer Experience Coach

The Ideal Speaker for Your Next Conference, Meeting or Training!

**Keynotes ✪ Conferences ✪ Spice up a Meeting
Training Seminars ✪ Team Coaching ✪ Special Events
College and Student Programs**

For more information on his inspiring topics on Leadership, Customer Service, Team and Sales Relationships, Customer Experience Makeover Programs, or to check availability to create magical results in your business or organization, contact:

JOHN FORMICA

Motivational Speaker * Team Coach

(704)965-4090

info@johnformica.com

www.johnformica.com

I Would Love to
Hear from *You*!

If you have a story about a *Magical Customer Experience* received from a business or employee;

If you have a story about a *Magical Relationship* that was created from a business or organization;

If you have examples of how you or other companies create a *Fun* environment in the workplace;

If you want to let me know what you or your small business is doing differently as a result of reading this book;

OR

If you would simply like to tell me what you think about *Making the Customer Experience Magical NOW!,* and sign up for my free weekly *Magical Moment Minute* e-mail, I would love to hear from you!

Here is my contact information:

John Formica
John Formica Enterprises, LLC
phone: (704) 965-4090
email: info@johnformica.com
Web site: www.johnformica.com

CPSIA information can be obtained at www.ICGtesting.com
Printed in the USA
BVOW080703090413

317630BV00001B/2/P